WHAT A FUCKING DAY

Funny Adult Coloring Book
for dealing with today's bullshit

DOODLESKULL

NOTE

This coloring book contains
sayings with swear words
and occasionally, humor.

This book intended for
lightening up your day,
not for causing harm.

So pick up this book when
you find yourself thinking
"What a fucking day".

Let all that bullshit out
in your favorite colors.

This book contains
adult language
and is not intended
for children.

COPYRIGHT

ISBN

ISBN-13: 978-1535005098
ISBN-10: 1535005092

DEDICATION

This coloring book is dedicated
to you dear colorist,
who likes to color books
to forget stress and
all other shit.

You, who likes to laugh and
who has excellent taste
in humor.

This book
is for you.

Enjoy.

This coloring book is colored by:

_____

COLOR TEST PAGE

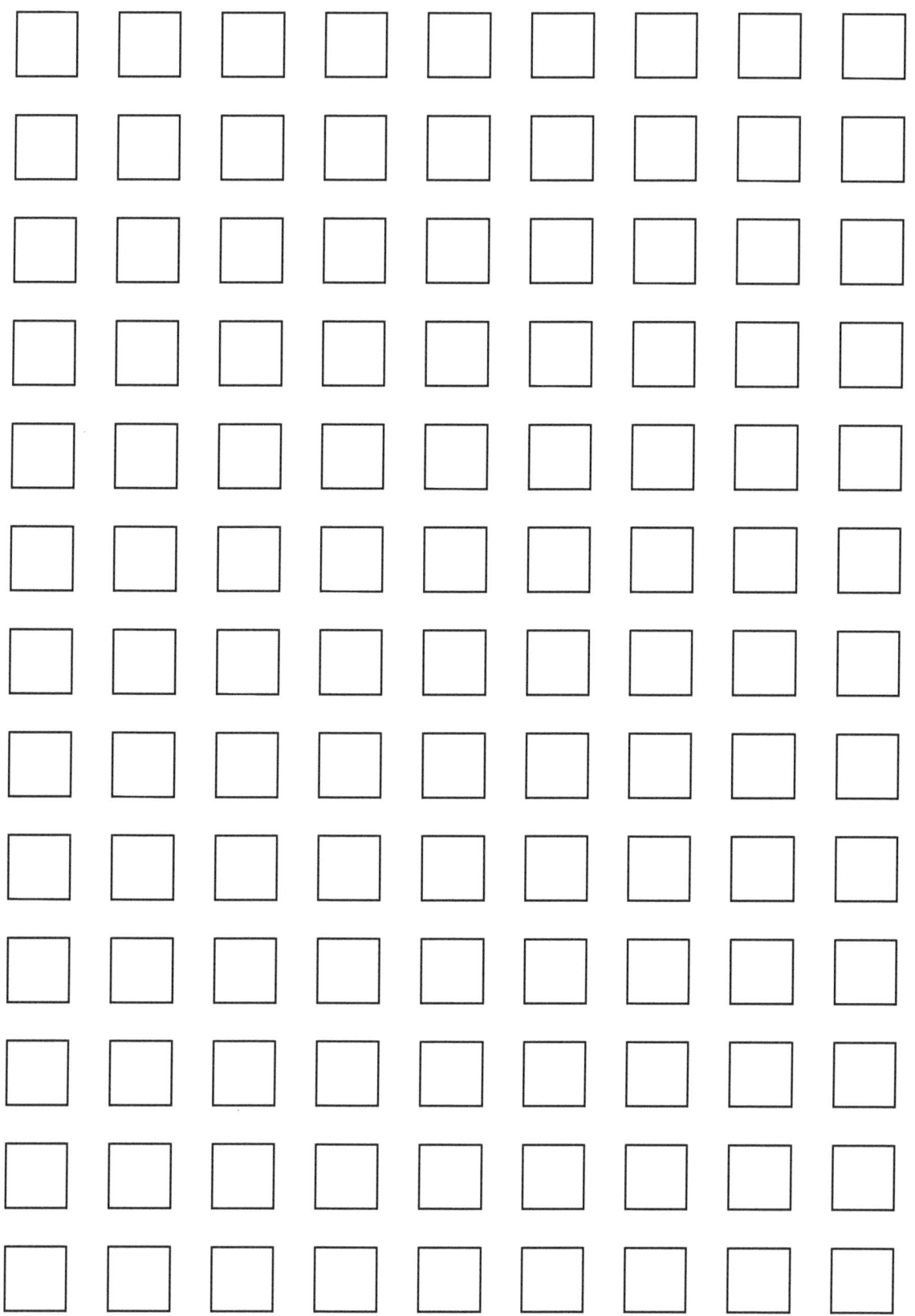

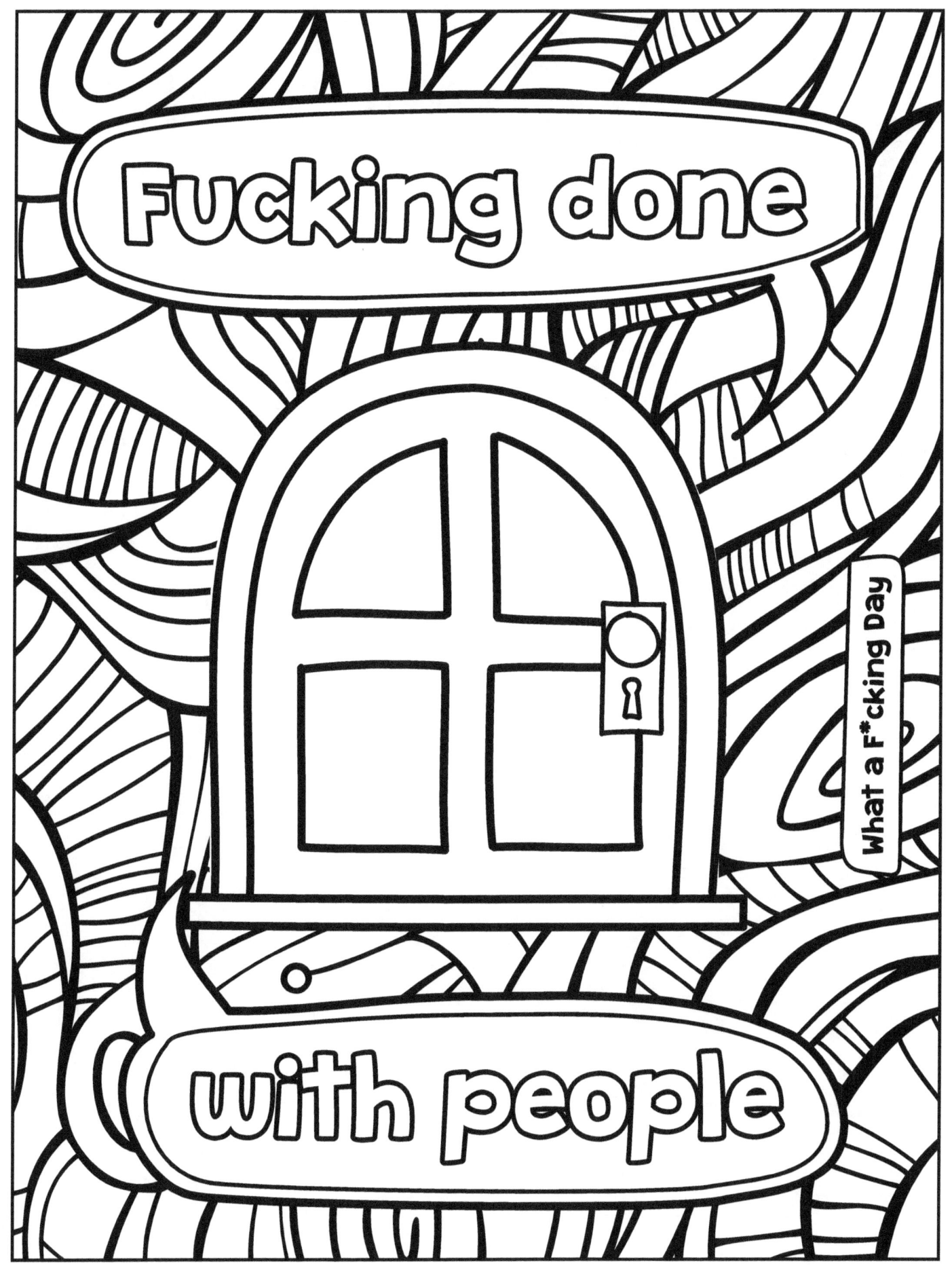

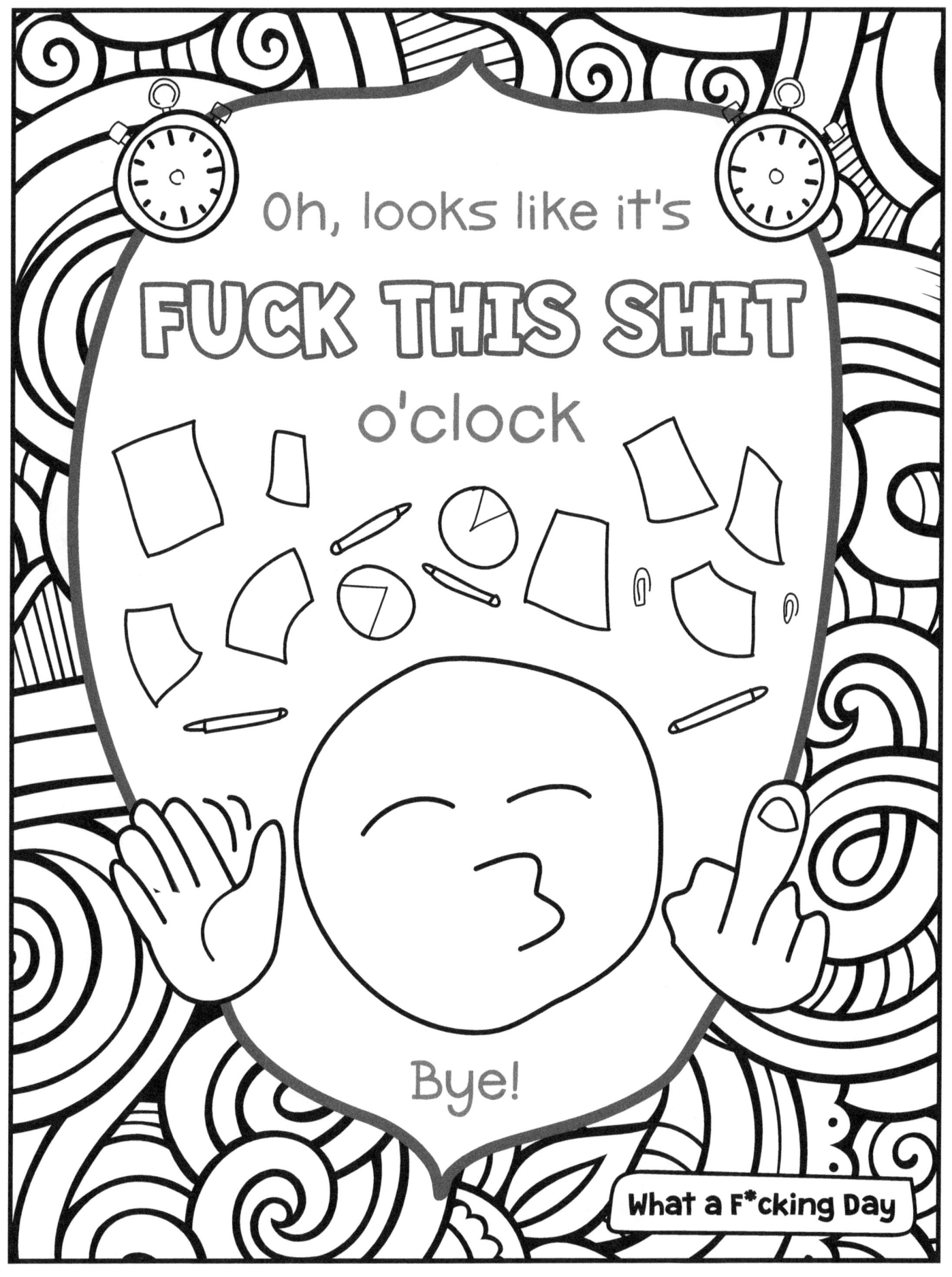

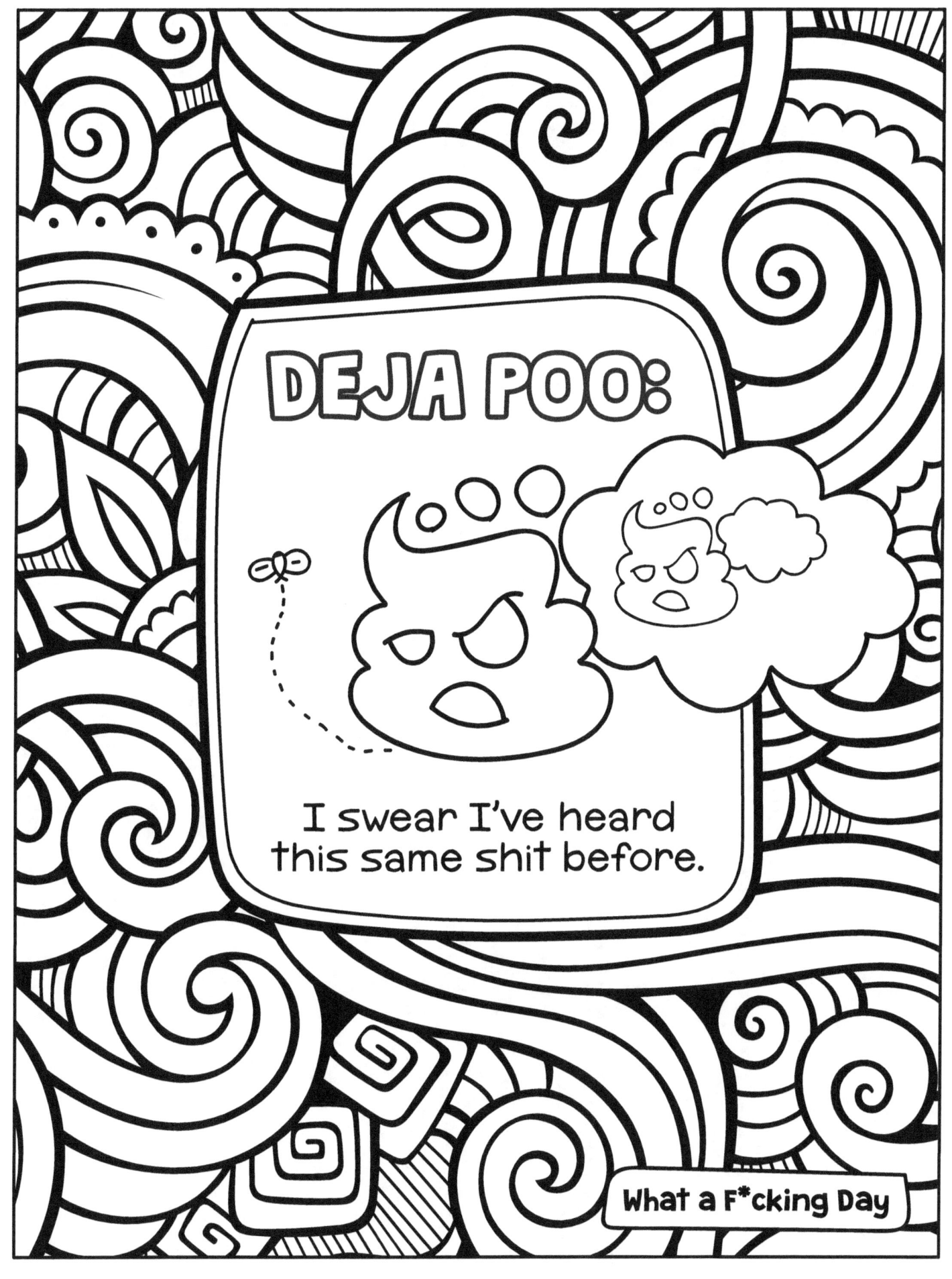

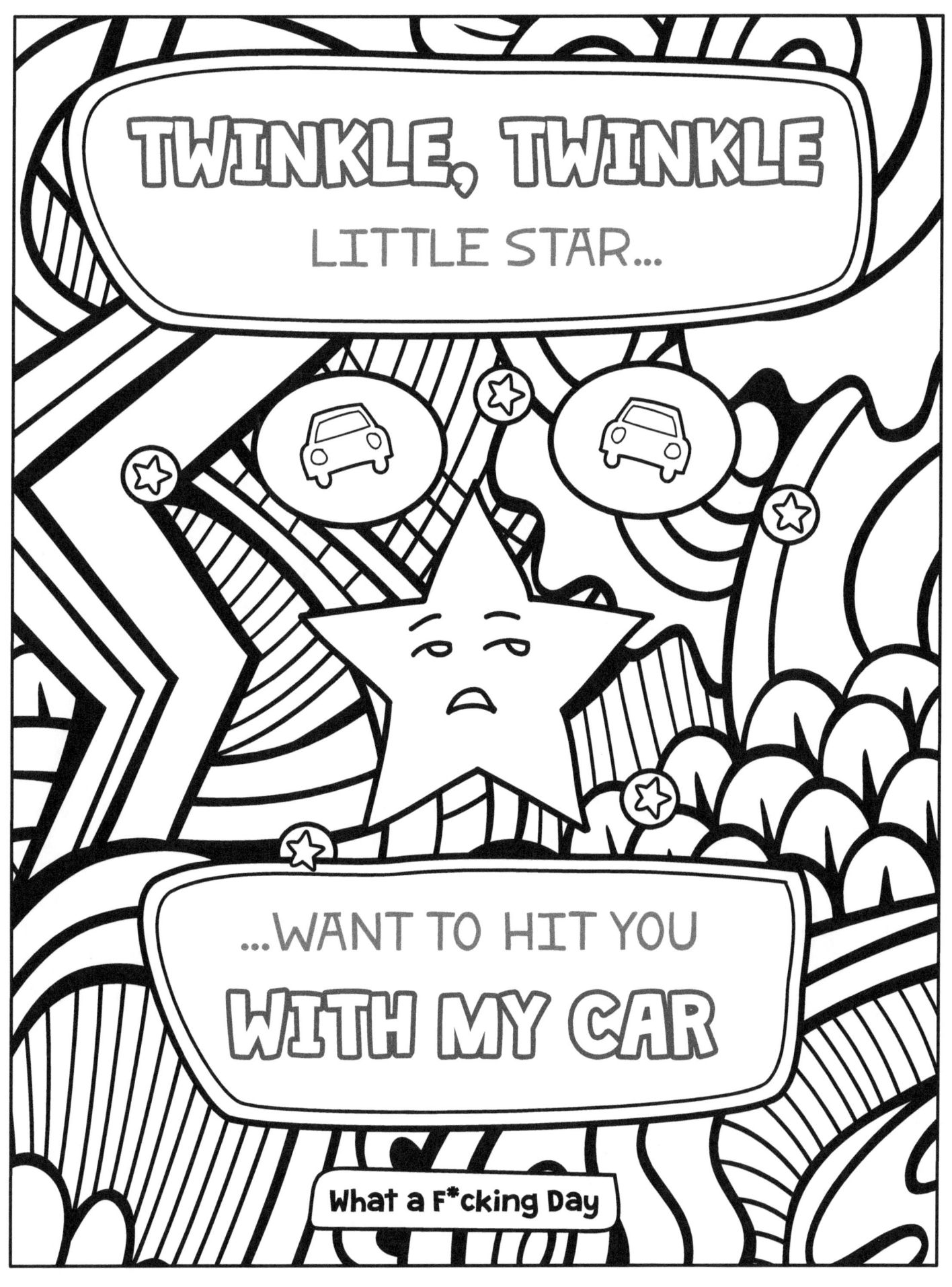

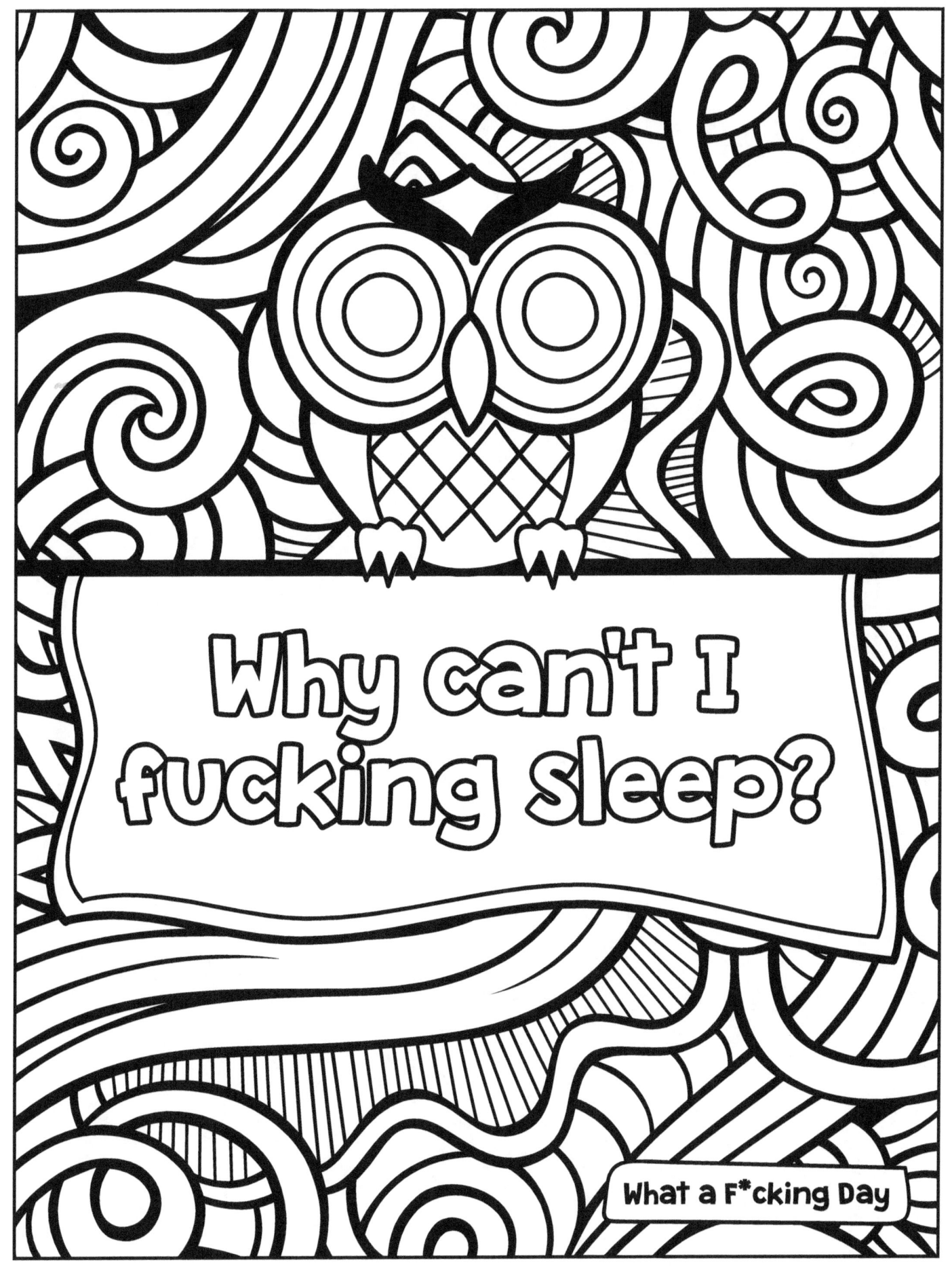

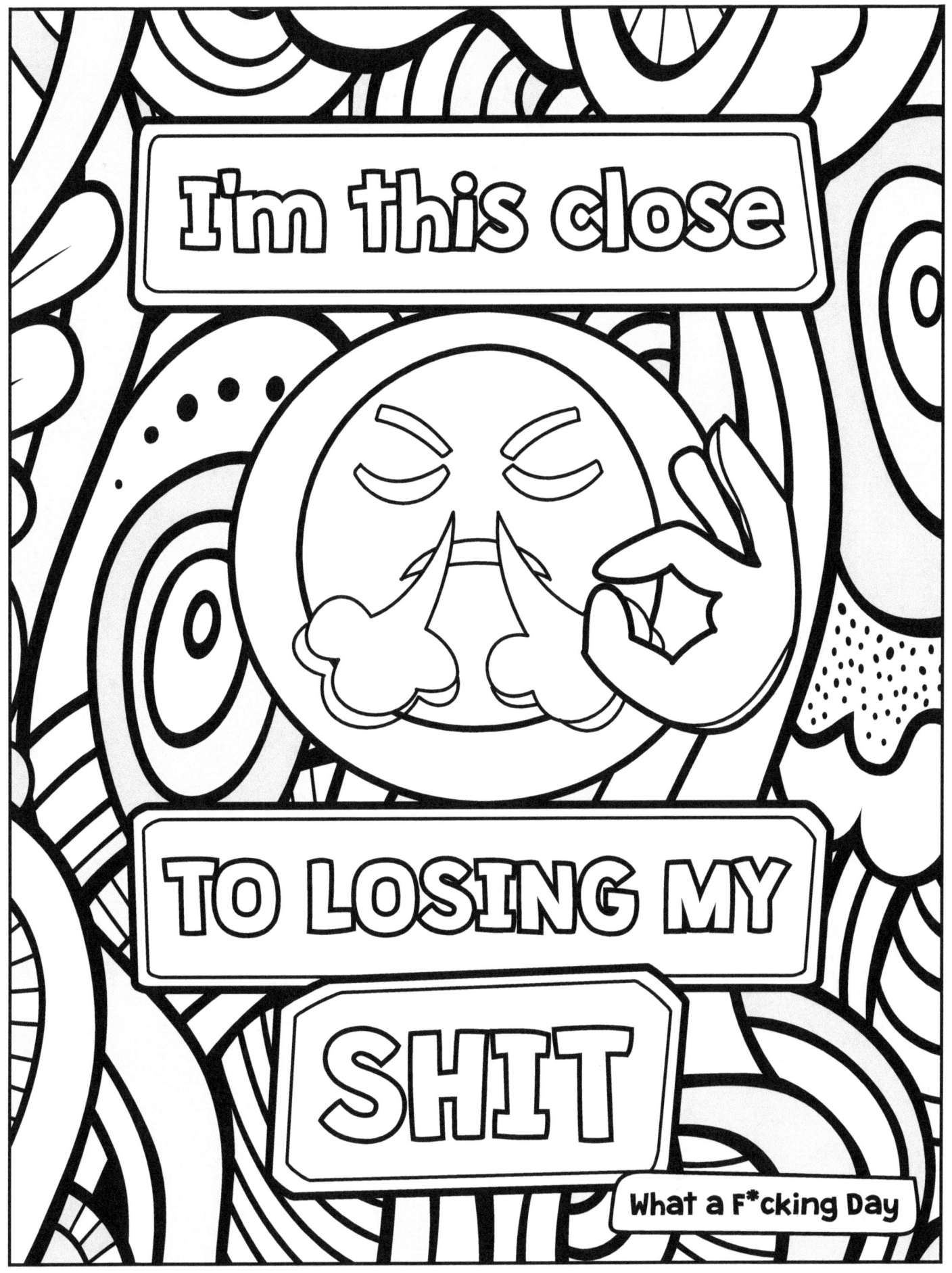

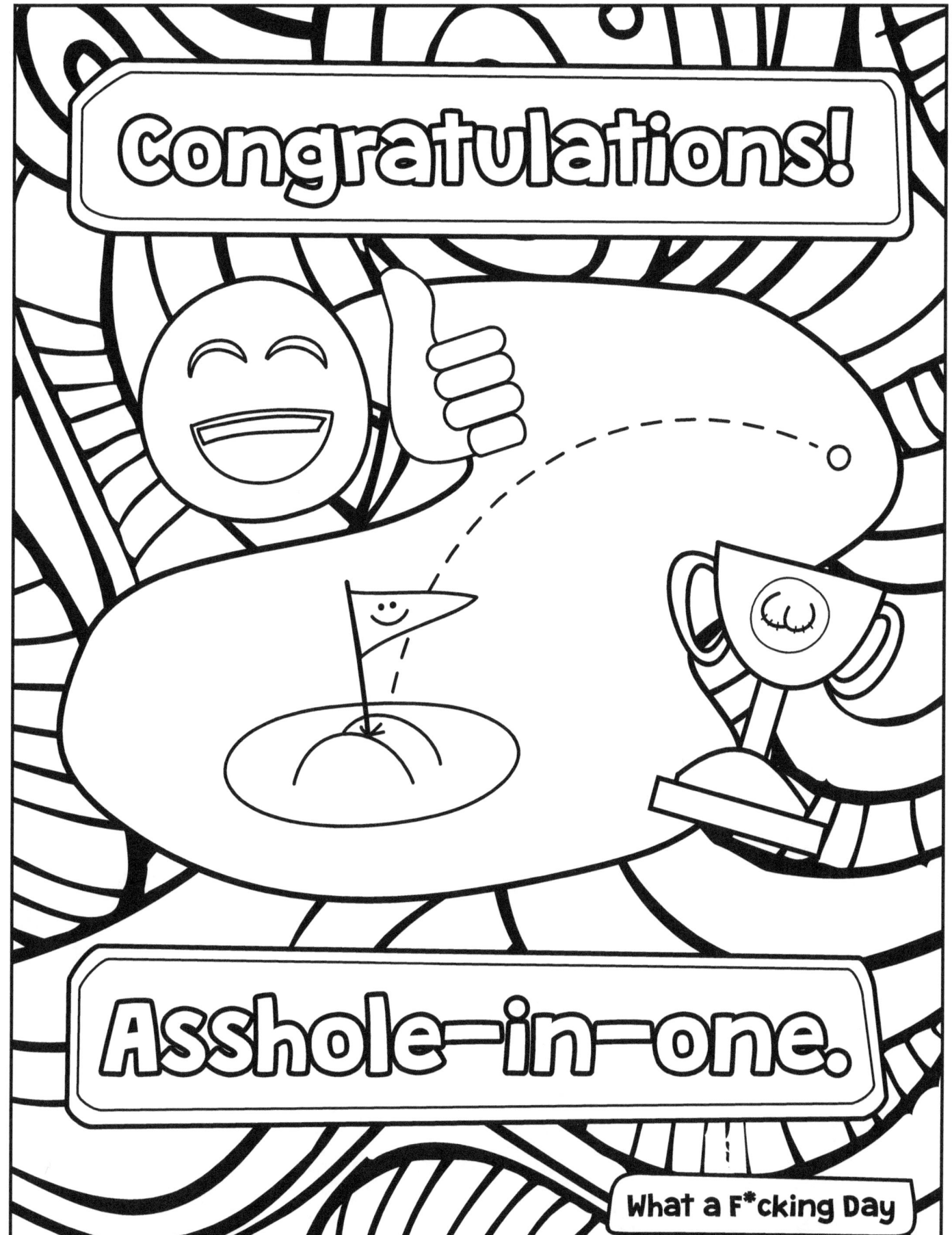

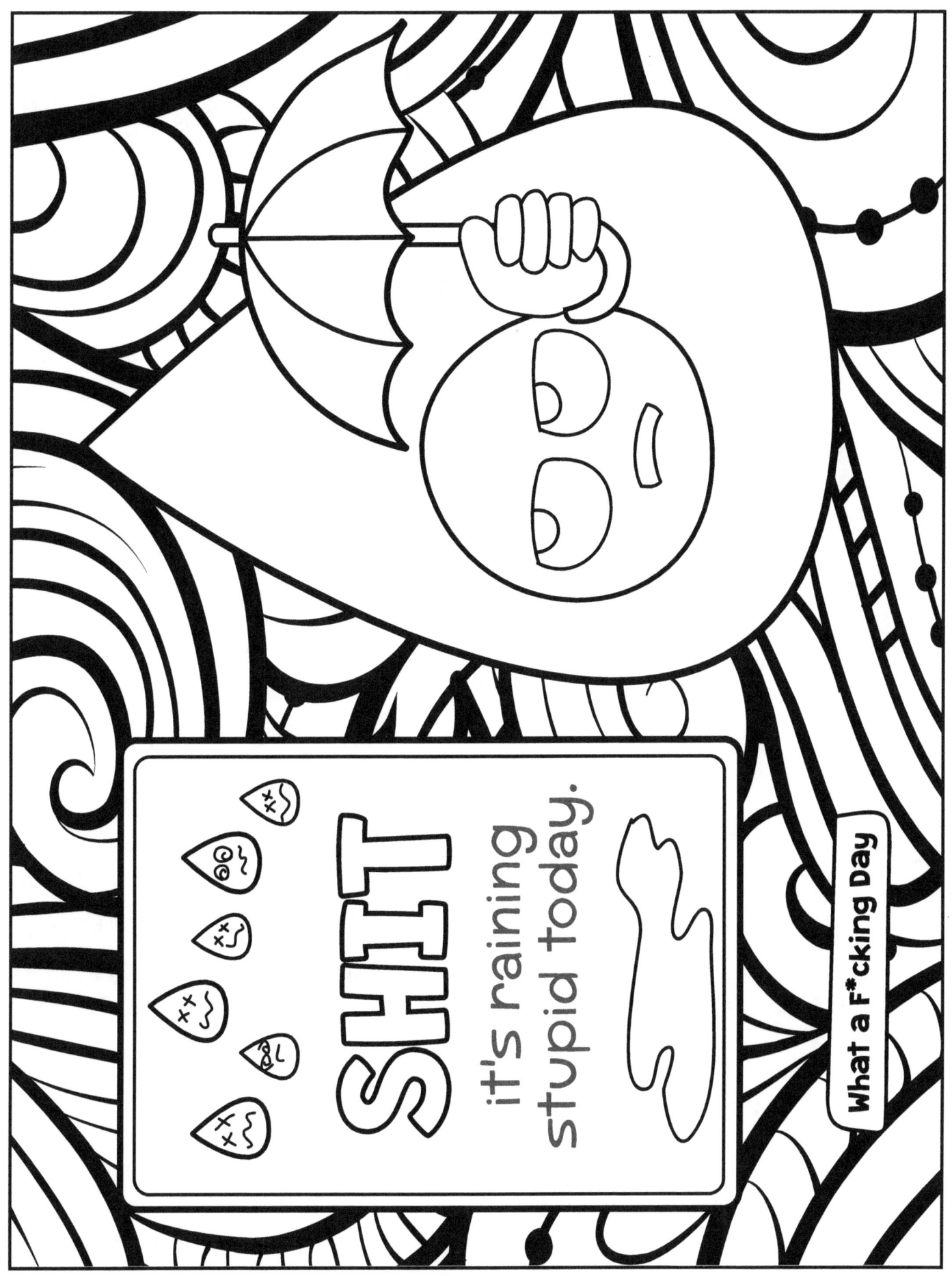

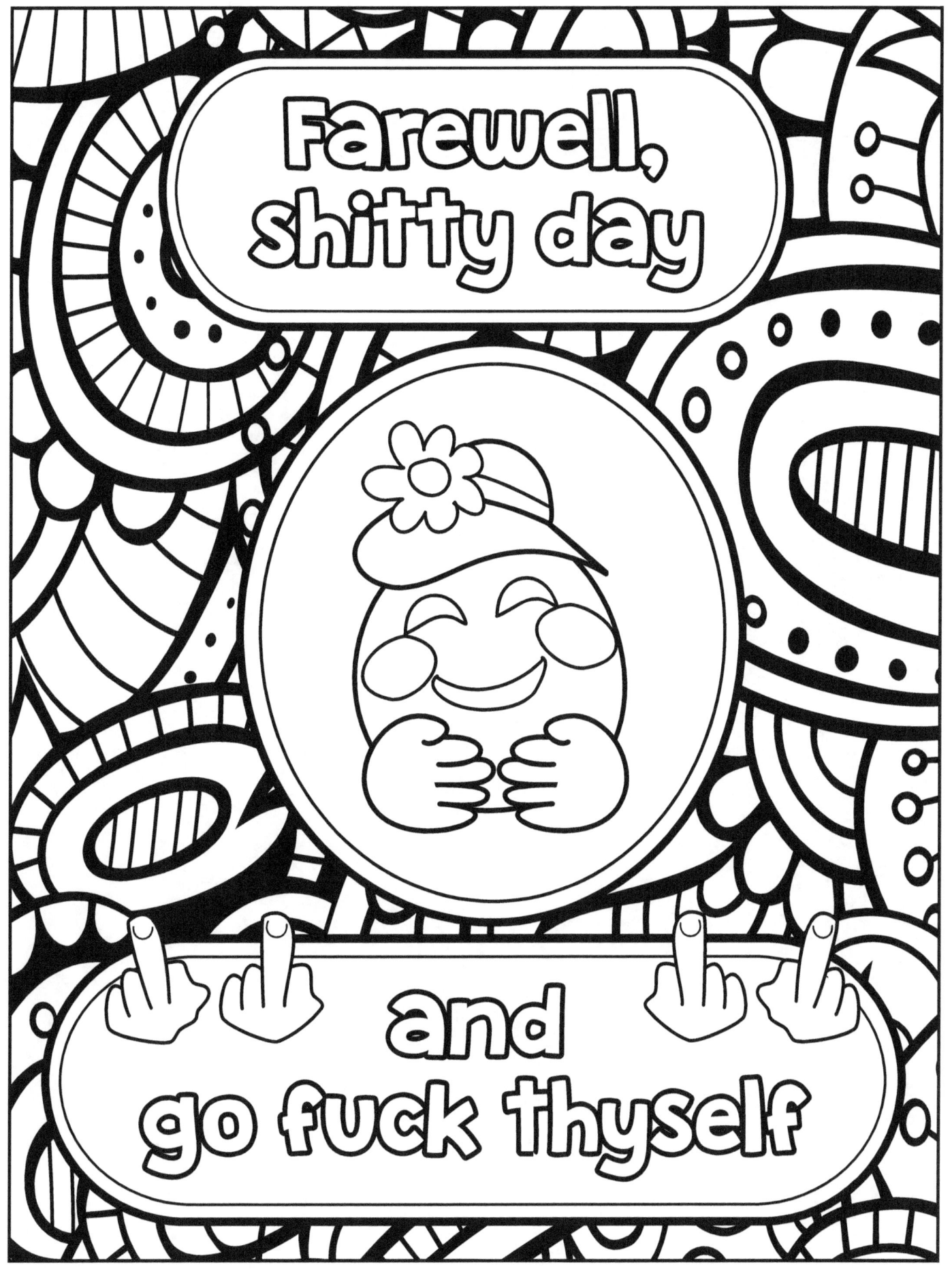

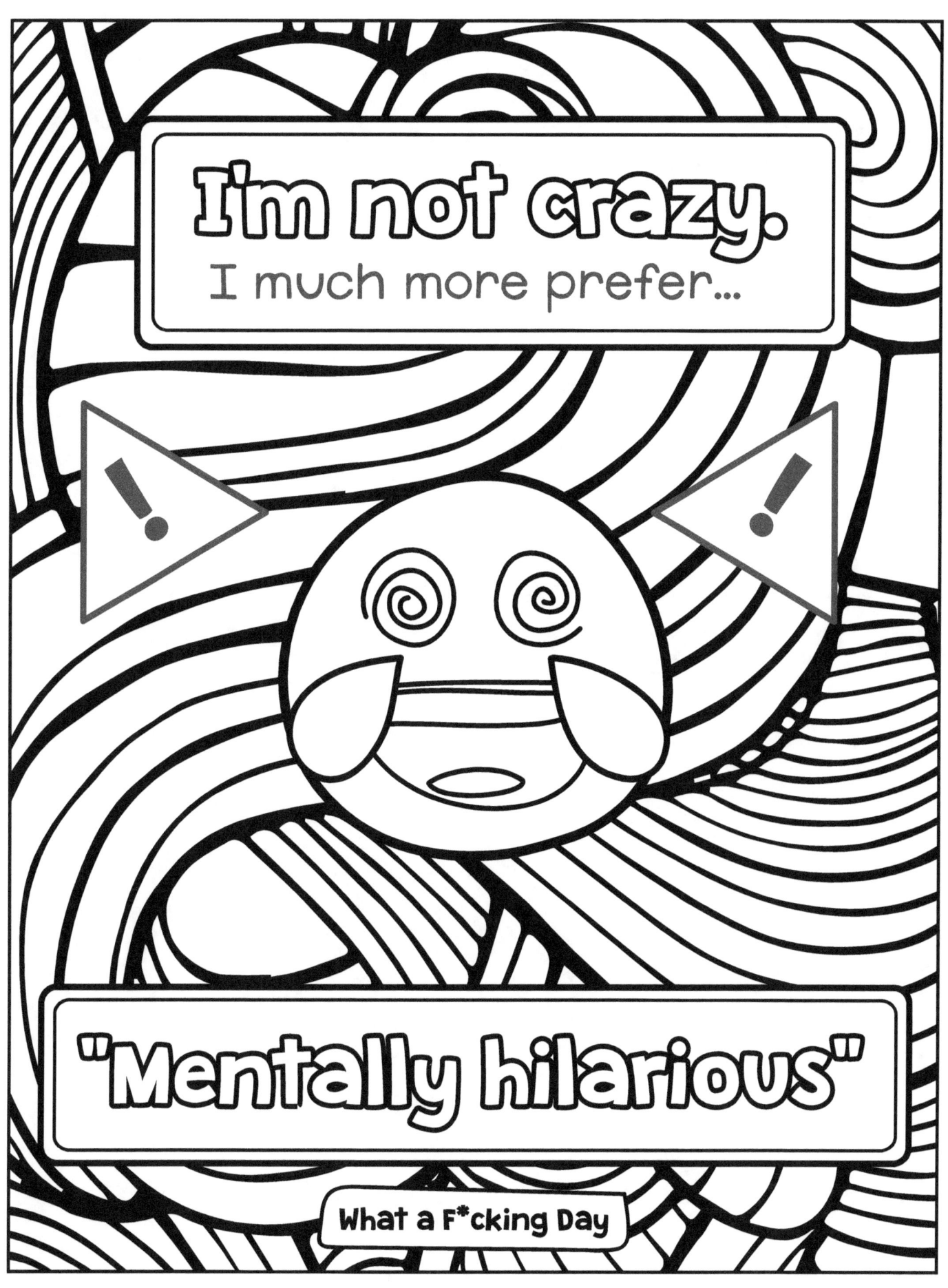

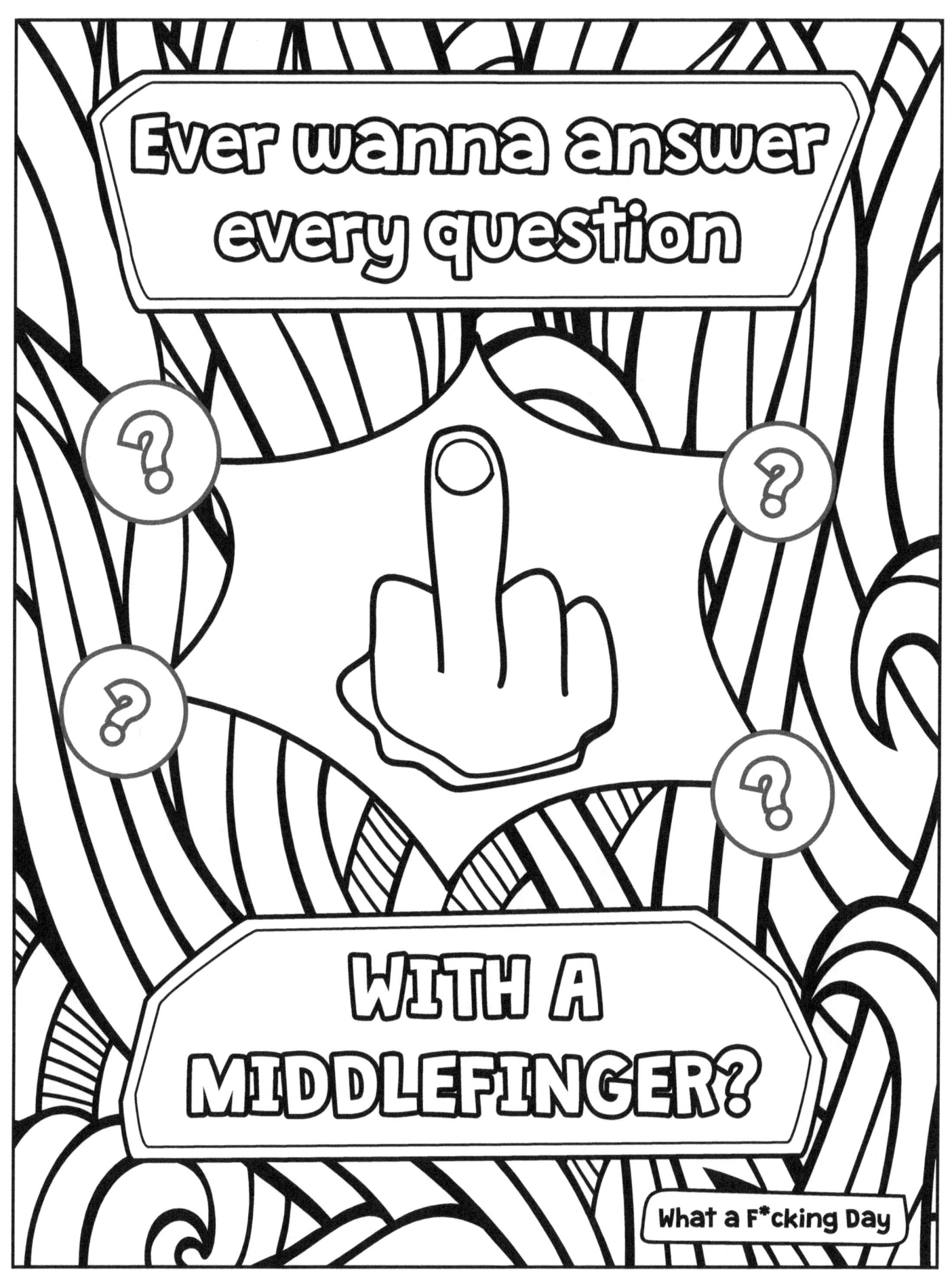

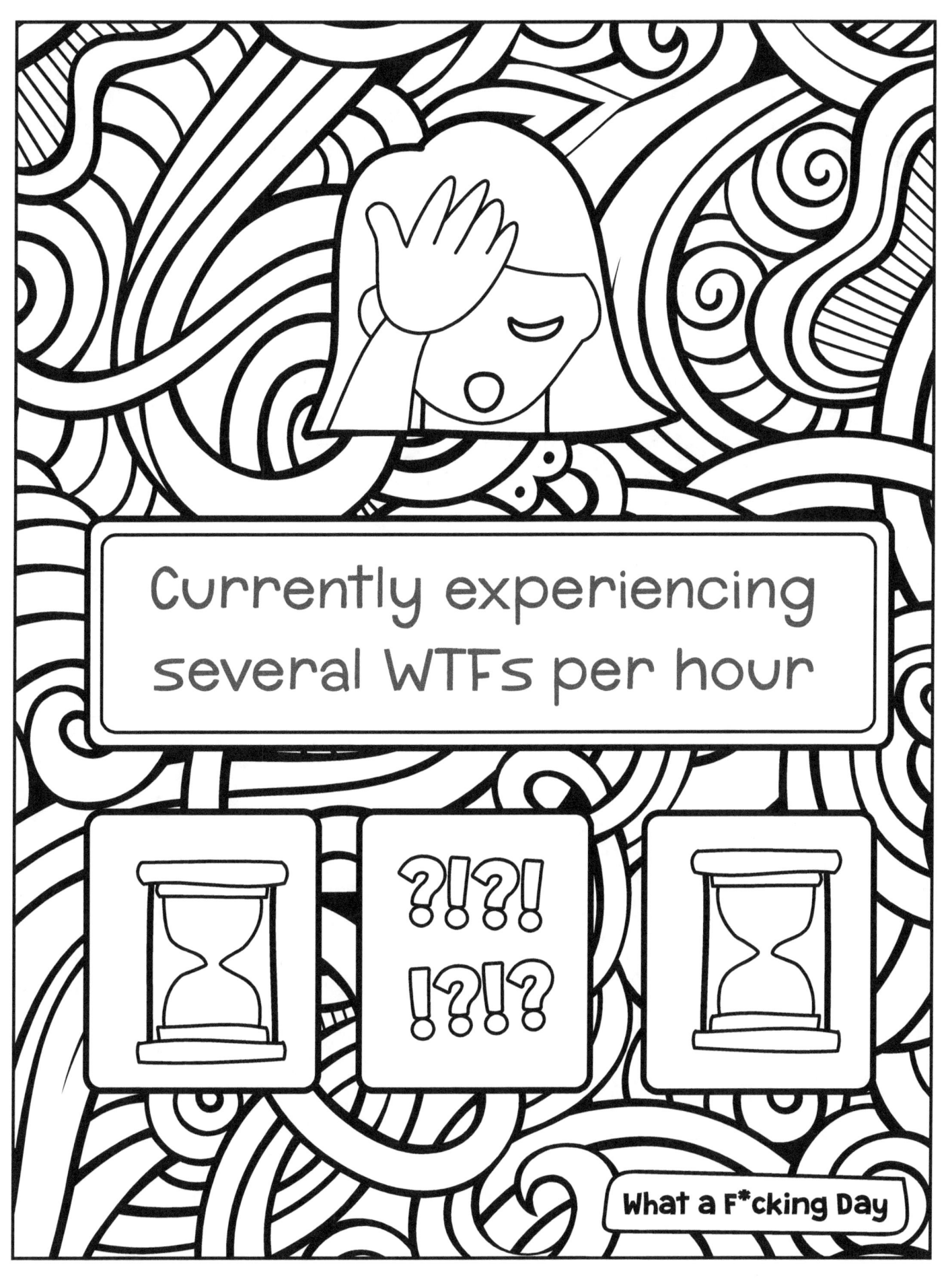

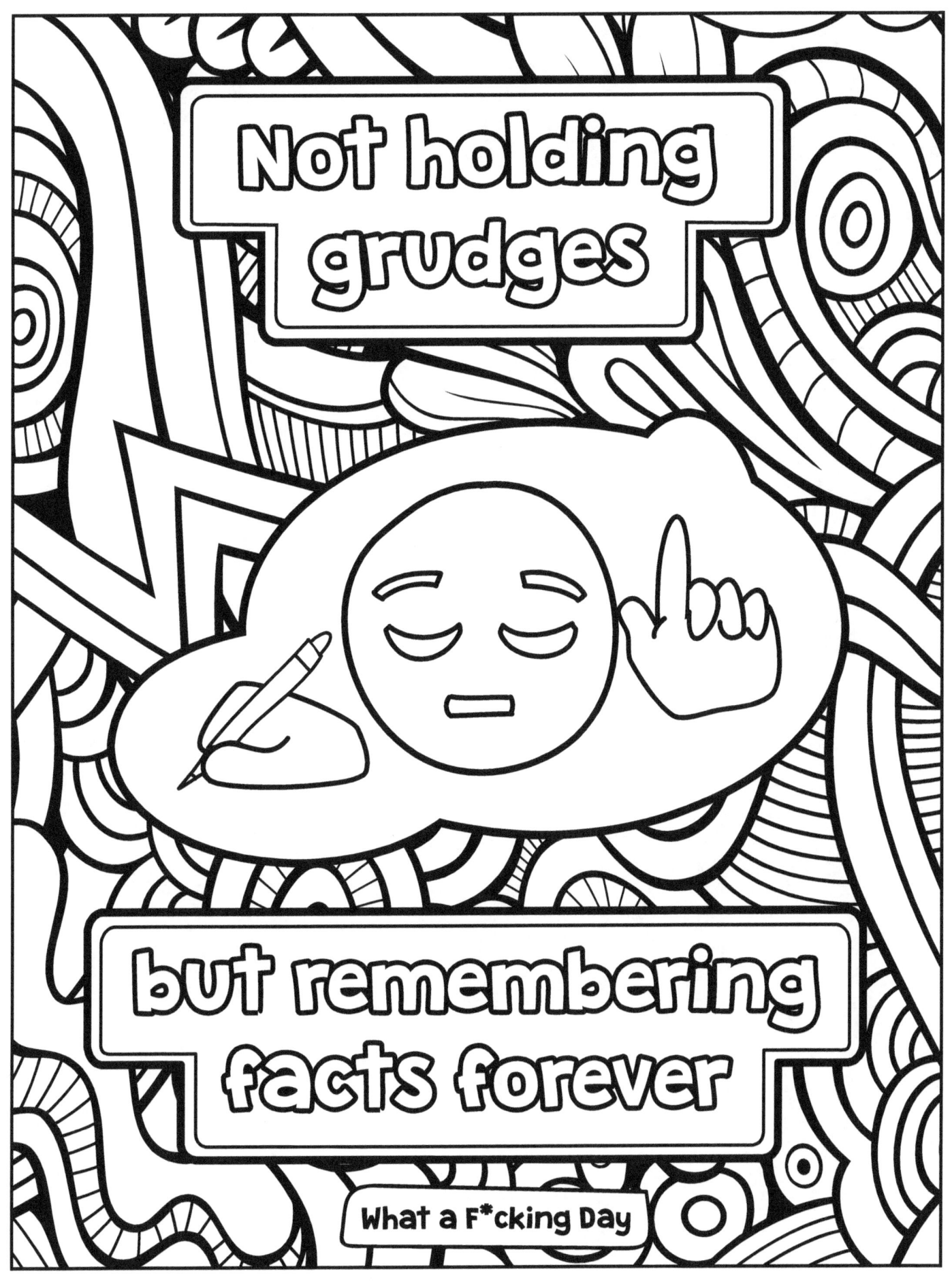

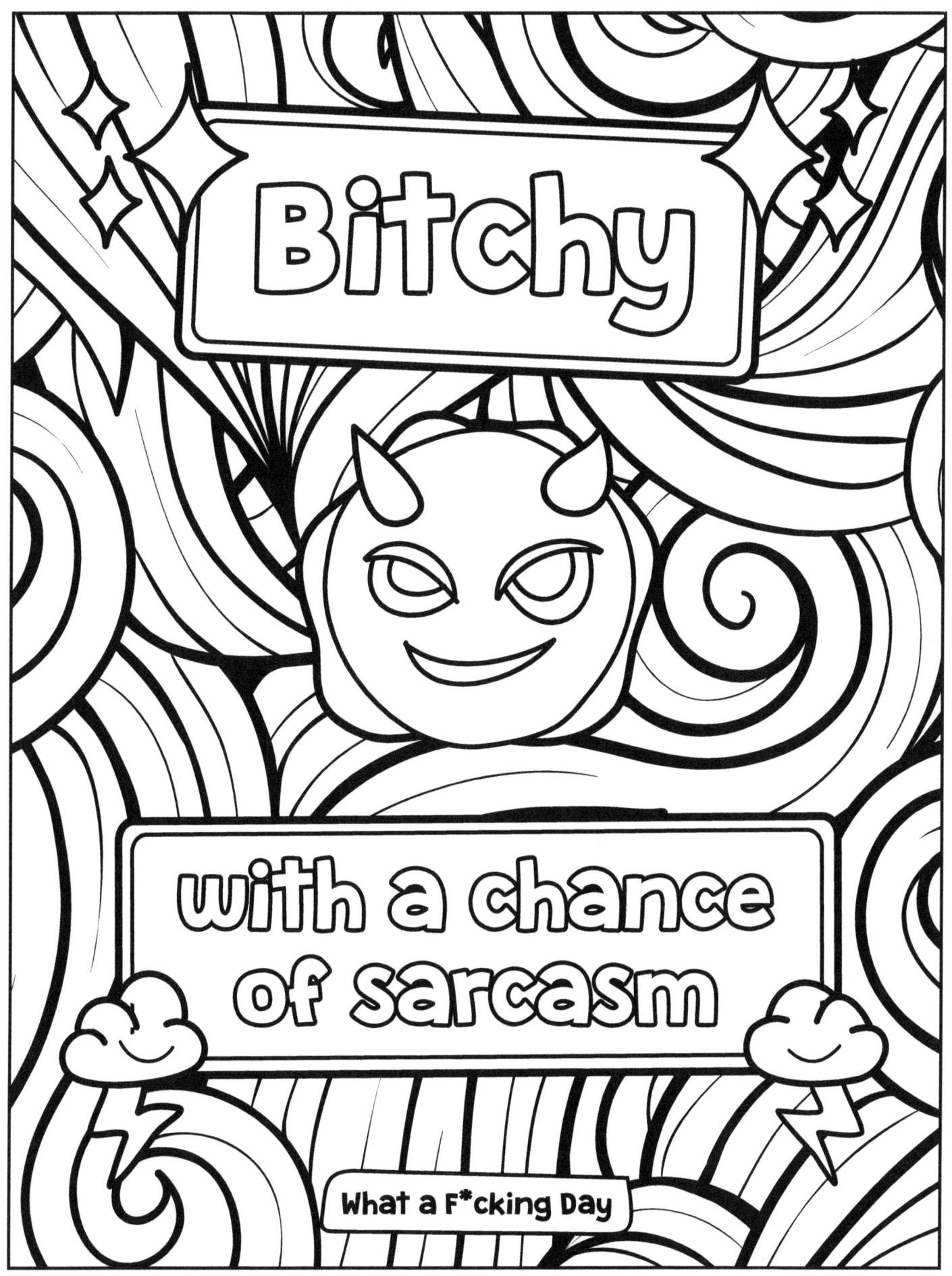

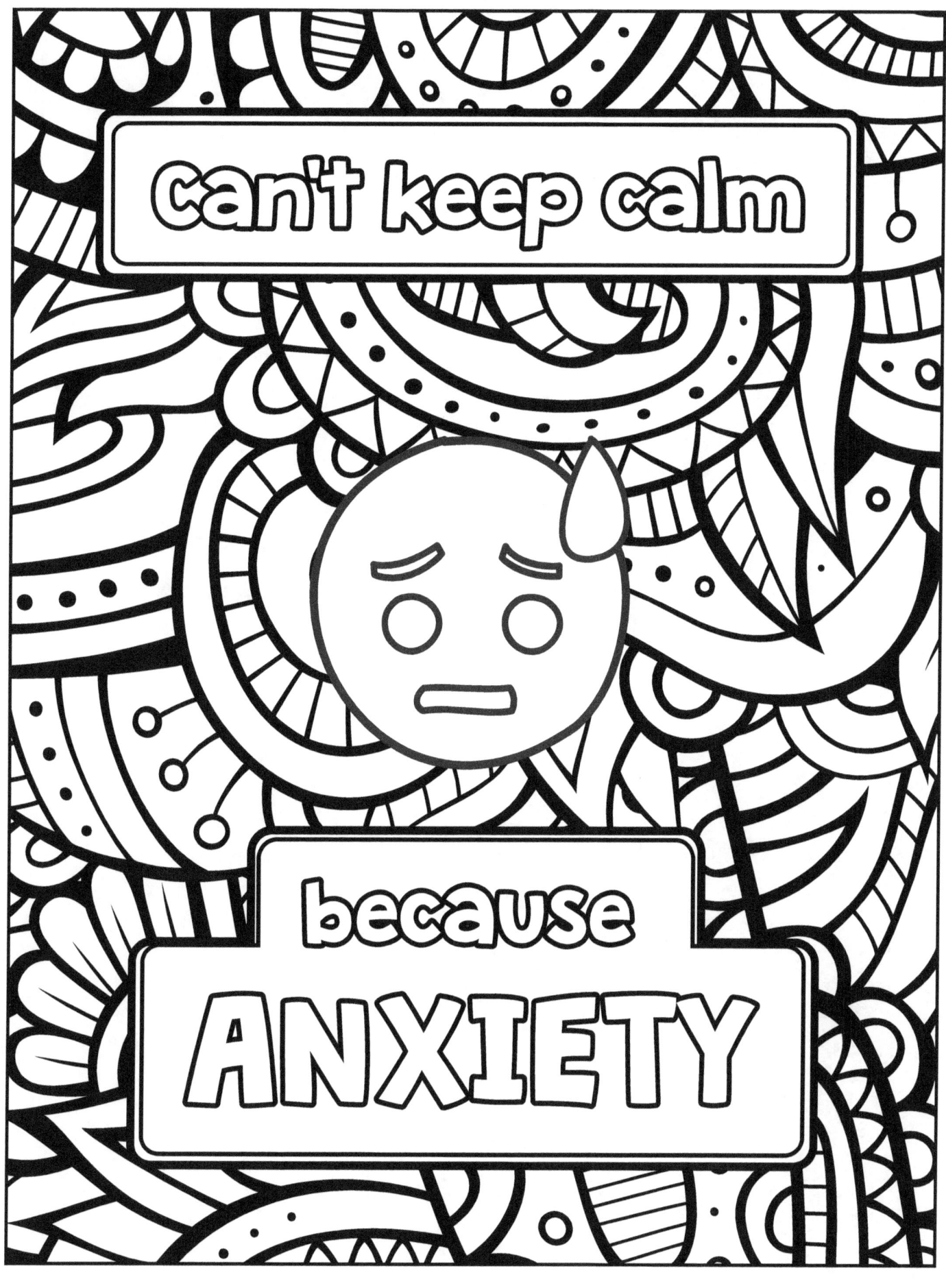

can't keep calm

because I

ANXIETY

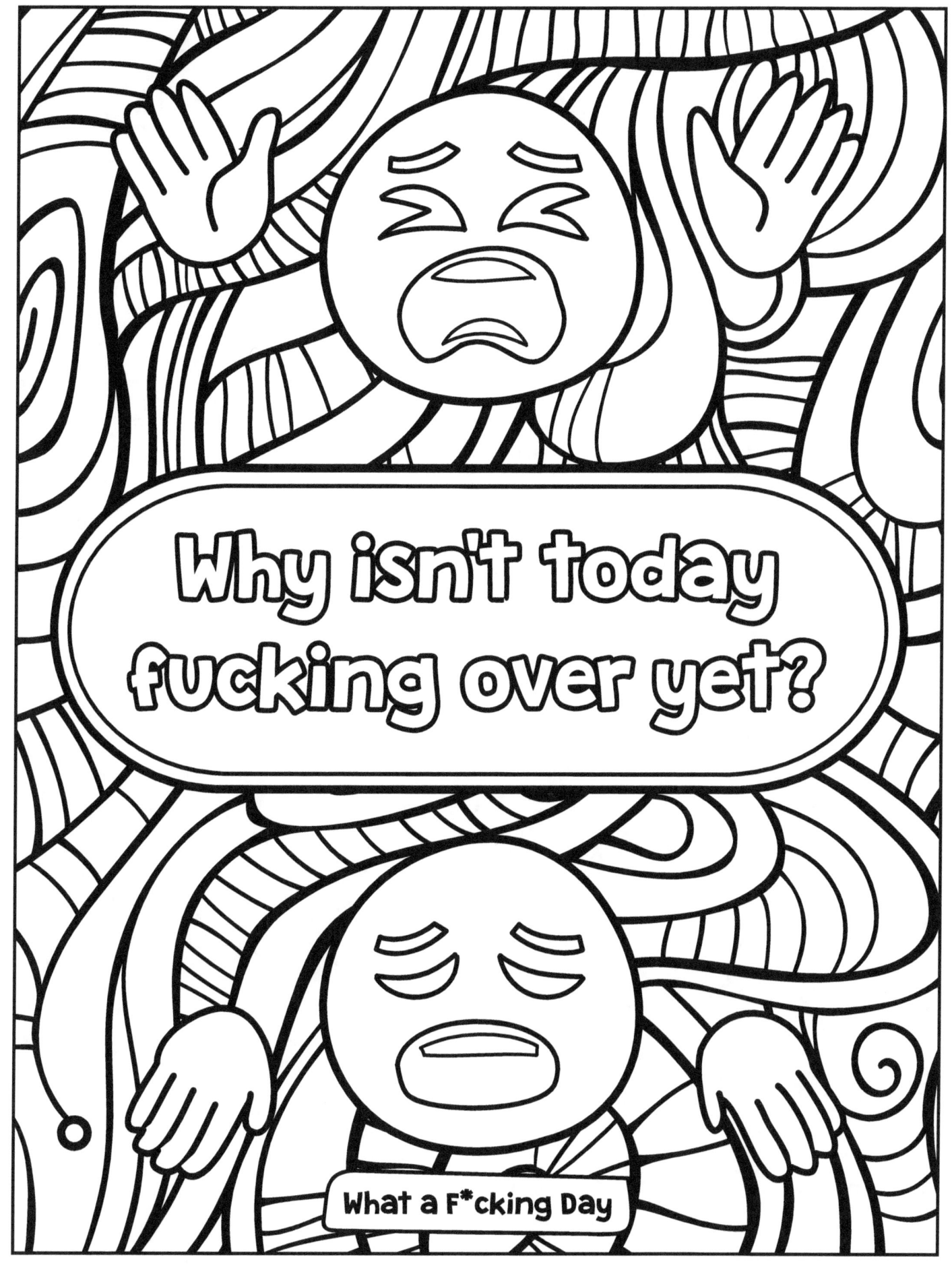

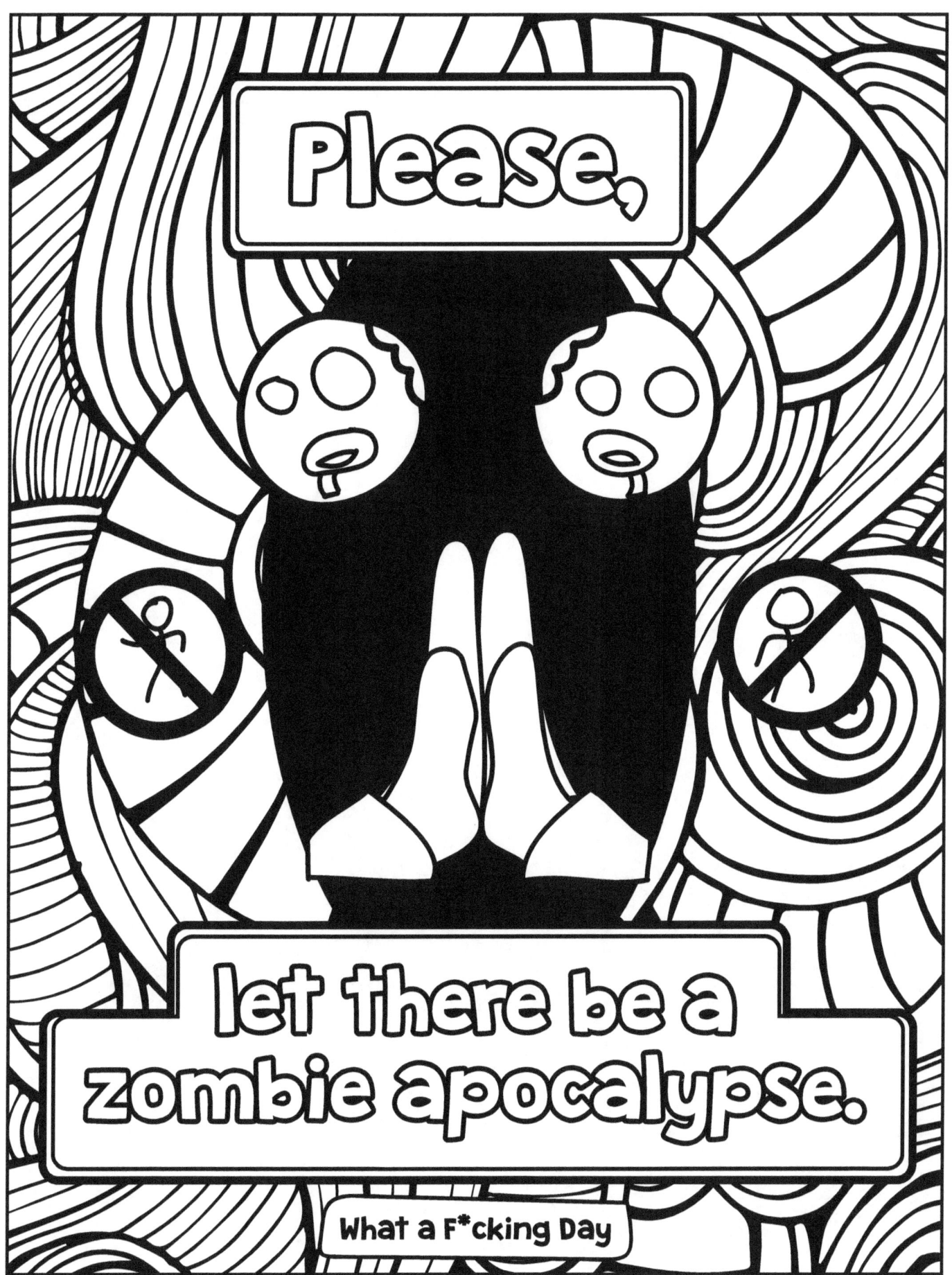

Please,

let there be a
zombie apocalypse.

what if I enjoy this day

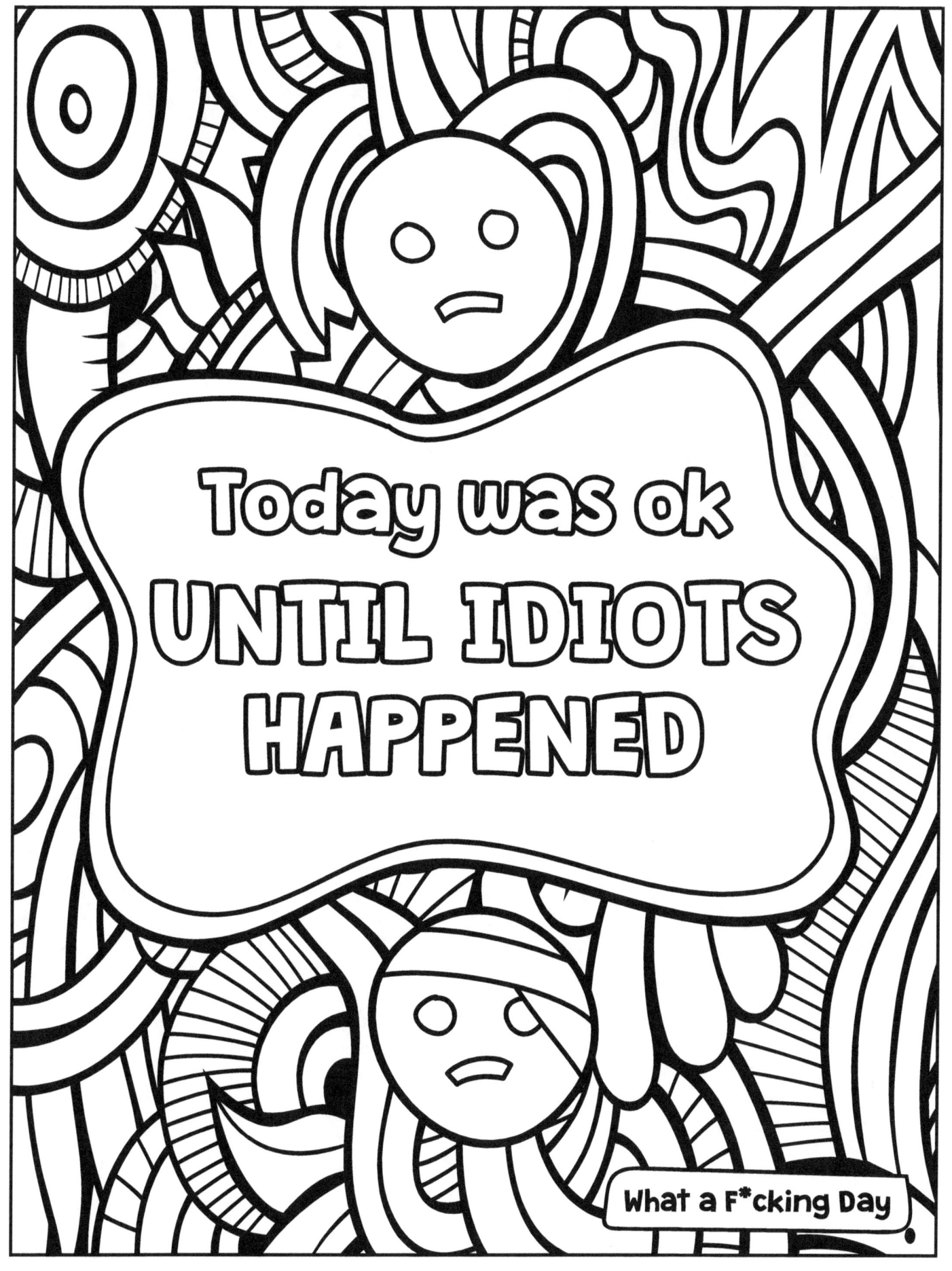

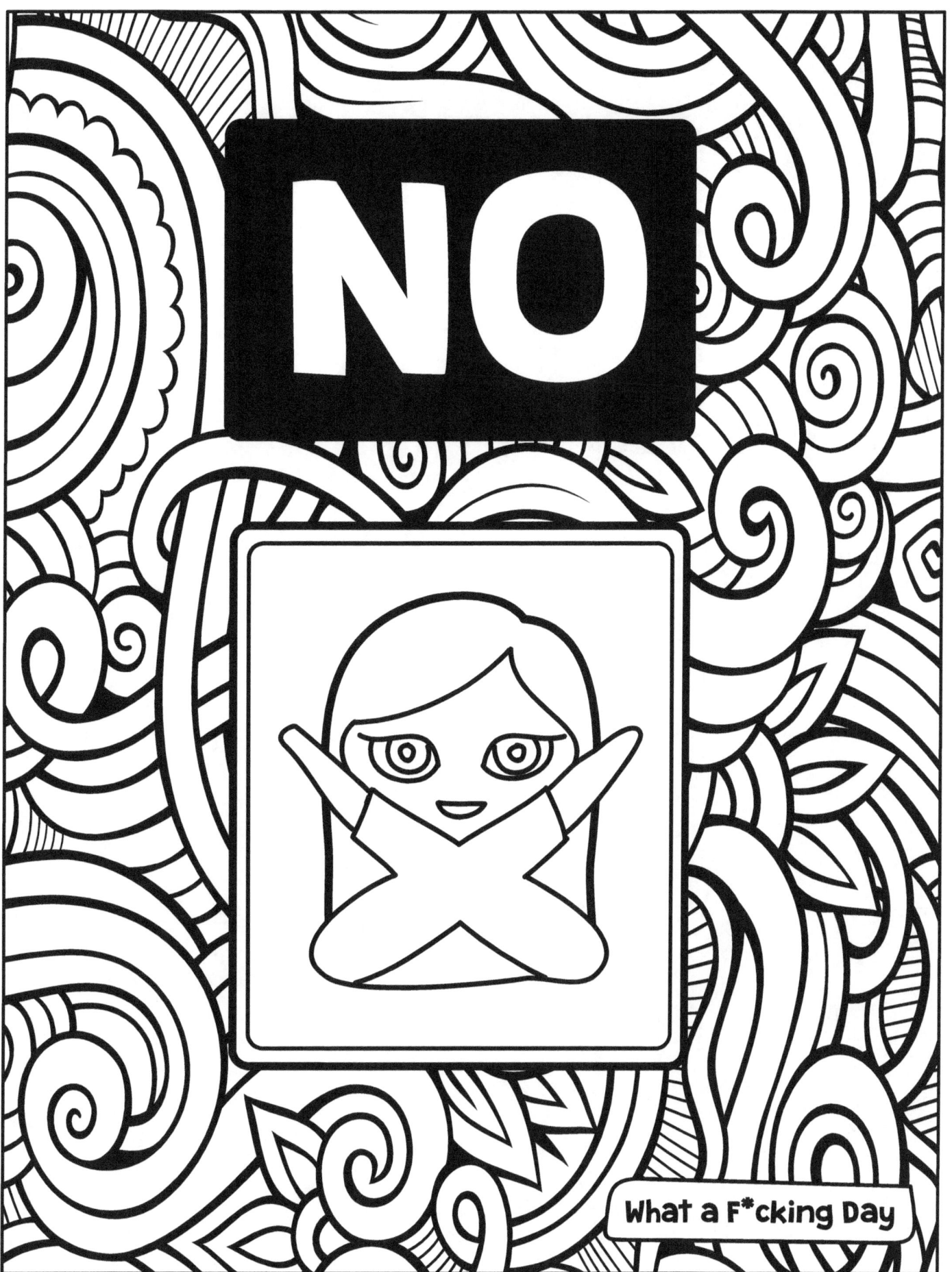

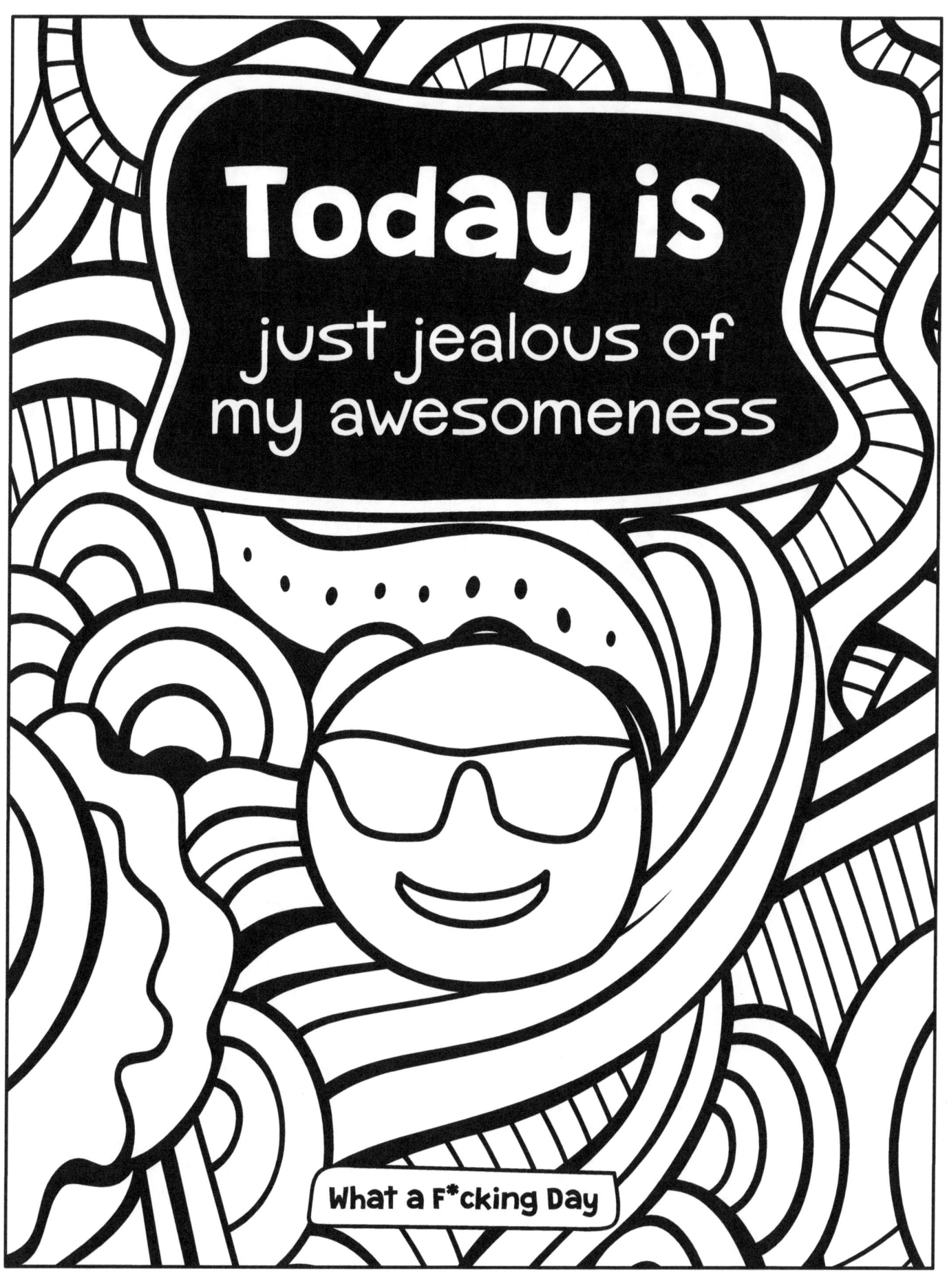

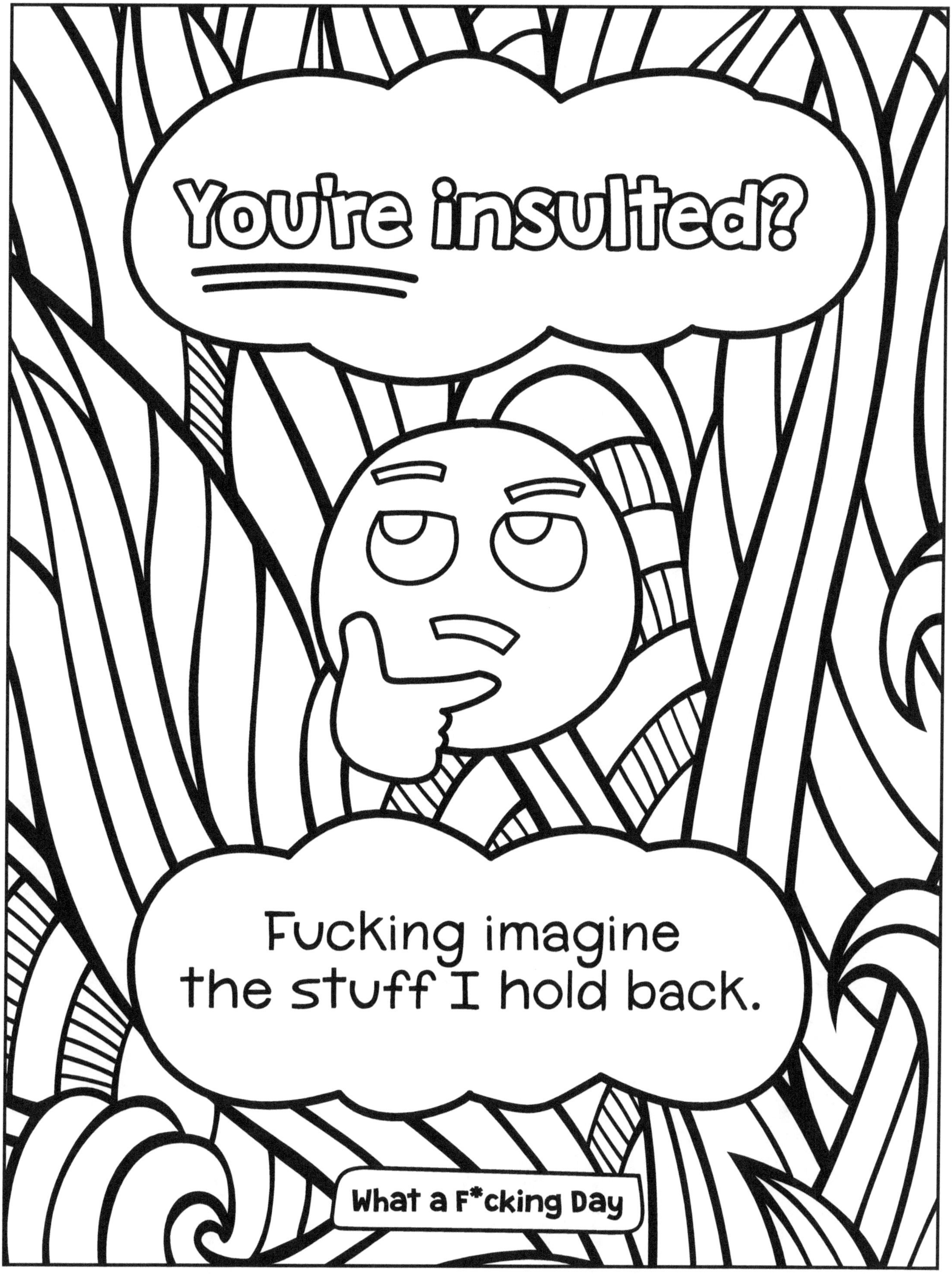
You're insulted?
Fucking imagine the stuff I hold back.
What a F*cking Day

PAGE OF THANKS

This book wouldn't be possible
without these special people:

Erica Lesley-Thigpen
Sarah Stephens
Craig Powell
Diana Perry
Hannah Kettle Mitchell
Nancy Graham
Shawna Collins
Megan Page
Ashley Appleyard
Nikki Davis
Bridget Hammer
Vandana Rampersad
Lisa Fodor-Randazzo

You helped me with this book
from beginning to the end,
and I owe a huge thanks for
the incredible of support
I've gotten from you.

Thank you.

www.ingramcontent.com/pod-product-compliance
Lightning Source LLC
Chambersburg PA
CBHW080559190526
45169CB00007B/2824